W9-BYA-804

French Bulldog

The Frenchie

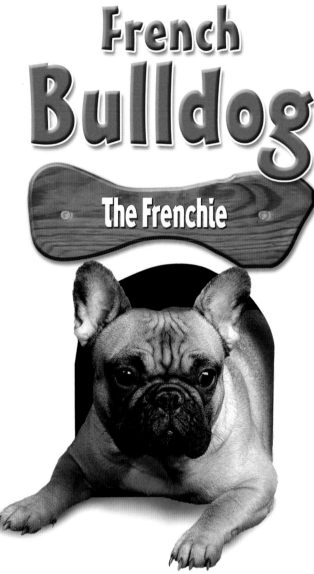

by Joyce Markovics

Consultant: Jan Grebe
President, The French Bull Dog Club of America

BEARPORT
PUBLISHING

New York, New York

Credits

Cover and Title Page, © Ira Bachinskaya/iStockphoto; TOC, © ingret/Shutterstock; 4, © Wildlife GmbH/Alamy; 5, © Tony Charnock/Alamy; 6, © Trinity Mirror/Mirrorpix/Alamy; 7, © Mirrorpix/Newscom; 8, © Juniors Bildarchiv/Alamy; 9, © RIA Novosti/Alamy; 10L, © The Granger Collection, New York; 10R, Bouboule de Madame Palmyre by Toulouse Lautrec/All Rights Reserved: Musée Toulouse Lautrec, Albi, France 11L, © Natalia V. Guseva/Shutterstock; 11R, Courtesy of Jan Grebe/FBDCA Magazine; 12, © Tony Anderson/Stone/Getty Images; 13, © Michelle V. Agins/The New York Times/Redux; 14, © Justin Black/Shutterstock; 15, © Sunny Lewis; 16, © Ira Bachinskaya/iStockphoto; 17, © Dorit Fischler/Belboulecan French Bulldogs; 18, © Rainer/blickwinkel/Alamy; 19T, © Rainer/blickwinkel/Alamy; 19B, © Jacana/Photo Researchers, Inc.; 20L, © M. Watson/Ardea; 20R, © Dorit Fischler/Belboulecan French Bulldogs; 21, © Rainer/blickwinkel/Alamy; 22L, © Motofish Images/Corbis; 22R, © fotototo/blickwinkel/Alamy; 23, © Connie Summers/Paulette Johnson/Fox Hill Photo; 24, © AP Images/The Martha Stewart Show; 25, © Robin Platzer/Twin Images; 26, © Kathi Liebe; 27, © Dorit Fischler/Belboulecan French Bulldogs; 28, © Jerry Shulman/SuperStock; 29T, © Eric Isselée/Shutterstock; 29B, © Eric Isselée/Shutterstock; 31, © Eric Isselée/Shutterstock; 32, © Medvedev Andrey/Shutterstock.

Publisher: Kenn Goin
Senior Editor: Lisa Wiseman
Creative Director: Spencer Brinker
Original Design: Dawn Beard Creative
Photo Researcher: Amy Dunleavy

Library of Congress Cataloging-in-Publication Data

Markovics, Joyce L.
    French bulldog : the frenchie / by Joyce Markovics.
        p. cm. — (Little dogs rock II)
    Includes bibliographical references and index.
    ISBN-13: 978-1-936088-21-8 (library binding)
    ISBN-10: 1-936088-21-5 (library binding)
    1. French bulldog. I. Title.
    SF429.F8M37 2011
    636.72—dc22
                            2010012999

For more information, write to Bearport Publishing Company, Inc., 101 Fifth Avenue, Suite 6R, New York, New York 10003. Printed in the United States of America in North Mankato, Minnesota.

072010
042110CGD

10 9 8 7 6 5 4 3 2 1

Contents

The Odd Couple

In 2000, Malone, a baby **orangutan**, was born at the Twycross (TWYE-krawss) Zoo in England. Within hours of his birth, the little reddish-brown ape was **abandoned** by his mother. Molly Badham, the zoo's director, was certain Malone would die if she didn't take action. So she took Malone home with her.

Some orangutan mothers raised in **captivity** reject their babies. Why? Many grow up without older females to teach them how to be good mothers. In the wild, there are many orangutan mothers to watch and learn from.

▲ **Like human babies, newborn orangutans need a lot of care.**

Bugsy, Molly's nine-year-old French bulldog, had been around zoo animals all his life. He usually never took an interest in the animals Molly brought home to care for—until Malone arrived. When Bugsy spotted the baby ape, he "started to nuzzle and lick the orangutan," Molly recalled. At that moment, Molly knew that a beautiful friendship had begun.

▲ **Molly Badham was one of the founders of the Twycross Zoo, which opened in 1963.**

Bulldog Babysitter

Bugsy cared for his ape friend as only a French bulldog could. He stayed close to Malone, licked his soft fur, and played with him. Bugsy was **patient** with Malone, even when the ape tugged on his tail. At night, Bugsy waited until Malone fell asleep and then curled up beside him. When Malone was strong enough to care for himself, he rejoined his ape family at the zoo.

◀ **Bugsy may look tough, but French bulldogs are known for being loving and easygoing.**

Adult French bulldogs usually weigh around 25 pounds (11 kg). Baby orangutans, on the other hand, weigh only 3 to 4 pounds (1.4 to 1.8 kg).

About a year later, Bugsy befriended another zoo baby—a tiny **bonobo** named Kia, who was also **orphaned** by her mother. Just as he did with Malone, Bugsy made Kia feel right at home in Molly's house, welcoming her with lots of doggy kisses.

◀ **Molly Badham and two bonobos**

Lap Warmers

It's no wonder Bugsy was such a loving friend. French bulldogs were **bred** to be **companions**. Frenchies, as they are also called, are related to the much larger English bulldog, which is now known simply as the Bulldog. In the 1800s, **lace makers** in England wanted a smaller version of the dog that could sit on their laps and keep them warm as they worked in cold workshops and factories. Over the years, they succeeded in breeding a friendly dog that was just the right size.

Frenchies got their start in Nottingham, England, more than 200 years ago.

◄ **An English bulldog**

During the **Industrial Revolution**, many of the lace makers moved to northern France for work. They brought their lovable **lapdogs** with them. By the late 1800s, the small dogs came to be known as *bouledogues Français*, or "French bulldogs."

Some people in England were upset that a dog originally bred in England came to be known as the Frenchie.

▲ **A lace maker at work**

Voyage to America

The small bulldogs grew to be very popular in France. At first, people such as butchers and café owners kept Frenchies as pets. Then wealthy people starting raising them, too. Before long, the sweet dogs captured the hearts of well-to-do Americans traveling to France. The Americans loved the little dogs so much that they took them back to the United States. By the end of the 1800s, the **breed**'s popularity was widespread.

French bulldogs were popular pets for the wealthy in the 1800s.

While Americans were bringing the dogs from France to the United States, British breeders took them back to England, the place where the dogs were originally bred.

The Frenchie was so popular in France that the famous artist Henri de Toulouse-Lautrec included a French bulldog named Bouboule in his art. Bouboule, shown here, was the dear pet of a well-known café owner in Paris.

The French, the Americans, and the British agreed that Frenchies were great pets, yet they couldn't agree on what the dog should look like. The French and British thought their pets should have "rose" ears, which are droopy and folded over. Americans wanted their dogs' ears to stand straight up, just like a bat's ears. So at the time, two different types of Frenchies were bred. Today, however, all French bulldogs have the distinctive "bat" ears.

▲ A French bulldog with "rose" ears

◀ A French bulldog with "bat" ears

City Pups

Today, the French bulldog is more popular than ever in the United States, especially in cities. Why? Their small size makes them a perfect pet for apartment living. Also, they are pretty quiet, except for the strange sounds that they're famous for making.

▲ Frenchies are small enough to easily ride in taxicabs with their owners.

"They don't bark," said Luke Herman, who owns a Frenchie named Jack and lives in New York City. "They have their own language of yodels, screams, chirps, warbles, and what can best be described as *snorfles*." Luke says that Jack often makes these sounds when he is playing with all the other Frenchies that live in their neighborhood.

Luke Herman's dog, Jack

Because of their short noses and pushed-in faces, French bulldogs don't breathe as easily as other dogs and often snort when they are playing. They also snore in their sleep.

Short and Stout

The bodies of Jack and his playmates are all built the same way—short and **stout**. A French bulldog's small muscular body is supported by strong bones. Their front legs are set wide apart, and their heads are large and square.

French bulldogs have large heads for their small body size.

French bulldogs may ▶ be small, but they have very strong bodies.

Cooper, a French bulldog from Montana, puts his big muscles to good use. For the last two years, he has competed in the Monster Dog Pull, a special weight-pulling contest. In 2008, Cooper pulled a sled that carried a 40 pound (18 kg) barrel a distance of 20 feet (6 m)—in just four seconds!

Cooper competing at a weight-pulling contest

Wrinkly Coats

While the strong bodies of French bulldogs make them stand out, so does their wrinkly skin. Frenchies have skin that is so loose it forms wrinkles. Most of the wrinkles appear on the French bulldog's shoulders and head. Many people think this just adds to their cuteness.

The deep wrinkles on a French bulldog's face should be carefully cleaned and dried to prevent **infections**. This should be done every week or as necessary.

▲ **Some Frenchies have serious skin problems that may cause them to lose their hair or to develop sores. Special medicine is needed to treat these problems.**

Their wrinkled skin is covered with smooth, soft, short hair that comes in a range of colors. However, some of the colors that are accepted by the **American Kennel Club** are **fawn**, **brindle**, cream, brindle and white, or white and fawn. The Frenchie's short hair is easy to care for, and the dogs should be **groomed** regularly.

▲ A black-masked fawn French bulldog (left),
a white and brindle French bulldog (center),
a dark brindle and white French bulldog (right)

Health and Care

Besides grooming, Frenchies also need to be taken to the **veterinarian** for regular checkups. The breed has some health problems that owners should be aware of. Their short noses and flat faces can make it hard for them to breathe. As a result, they have a tough time cooling down when it's hot outside, and can have a hard time catching their breath during exercise. To avoid this, they must be kept in a cool place on hot summer days. They should have access to shade and cold water even on milder days.

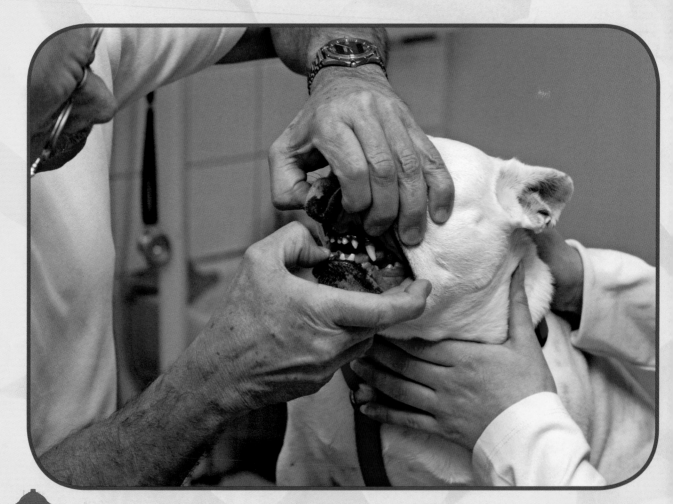

▲ **A veterinarian looks at a French bulldog's teeth.**

Some French bulldogs also have misshapen bones in their spines. The padding between these bones can break down, causing muscle weakness and pain. Other Frenchies may have problems with their hips and knee **joints**, which can become painful as they age.

A veterinarian checks out a French bulldog's hips.

French bulldogs should not be overfed. If they are fed too much, they can become overweight, which is very unhealthy.

Little Ones

Narrow hips make it hard for Frenchie mothers to deliver their puppies because the pups have very large heads. Females often need special surgery to help them give birth. Typically, there are three to five pups in a **litter**. A newborn usually weighs between eight and ten ounces (227 and 283 g)—that's about the weight of an orange.

◀ **Ten-day-old Frenchie puppies**

French bulldog puppies with their mother

Puppies feed on their mother's milk for up to six weeks. They start eating solid foods at around four weeks of age, which is when they become very active. Frenchie pups have loads of energy. Even at a young age, their playful personalities shine through.

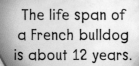
The life span of a French bulldog is about 12 years.

▲ **Five-week-old puppies eating solid food**

Clowning Around

Often described as clown-like, a Frenchie's playfulness continues through adulthood. Although French bulldogs can be silly and **mischievous**, they also have a strong desire to please their owners and to be a part of the family.

◀ Some owners enjoy dressing up their French bulldogs. The dogs don't seem to mind the silly costumes.

Although they are usually good with other dogs, Frenchies will sometimes try to defend their owners by growling at unfamiliar dogs.

Like all dogs, Frenchies require some training. From an early age, they should be taught to go to the bathroom outside, to walk on a leash, and to sit or stay. Alert and intelligent, French bulldogs learn quickly. Yet Frenchies can also be **stubborn** at times. Occasionally, owners need to gently remind their pets who's the boss. A good way for owners to do this is to sternly tell their dogs "no" when they are not behaving.

◀ **Though Frenchies don't need much exercise because of their small size, they should take daily walks.**

Martha's Dogs

Some of the most well-behaved and famous Frenchies around belong to TV show host Martha Stewart. Her two beloved dogs, Francesca and Sharkey, regularly appear on her television program, as well as on her popular website. The dogs even have their own website, called The Daily Wag, where stories are posted describing their adventures.

▲ **Martha Stewart and her French bulldogs Francesca (left) and Sharkey (right) on the set of her TV show**

Martha Stewart loves dressing her dogs up in special Halloween costumes. One year, Sharkey was a big white moth and Francesca was a scary black spider.

In addition to being a loving pet owner, Martha has helped educate people about the breed. On her website, she gives tips on caring for French bulldogs and provides information about their special needs.

◀ **Martha and her Frenchies**

Frenchie Fun

French bulldogs like to be with their owners whether it's in a television studio or at home. It's not uncommon for Frenchies to join their human companions on outdoor adventures. Kathi Liebe's Frenchies enjoy water sports. Dressed in their doggy **life jackets**, they love to ride on her family's **kayak**!

▲ **Kathi Liebe's husband, Al, kayaking with their Frenchies**

Most Frenchies are not able to swim. Their heavy bodies and big heads make it hard for them to stay afloat. For this reason, it's important that they wear life jackets in or around water.

Dorit Fischler's French bulldogs prefer snow to water. They join their owner on cross-country skiing trips in the snowy Canadian woods.

No matter the activity, French bulldogs are fun-loving, devoted pets. Many Frenchie owners couldn't imagine having a better friend or a more lovable **canine** companion.

▲ **Dorit's French bulldogs love to race and play in the snow.**

French Bulldogs at a Glance

Weight:	No more than 28 pounds (13 kg)
Height at Shoulder:	Between 12 and 12.5 inches (30.5 and 31.8 cm)
Coat Hair:	Short and smooth, with loose and soft skin underneath
Colors:	They come in many colors. Some of the colors recognized by the AKC are fawn, brindle, cream, brindle and white, or white and fawn
Country of Origin:	England
Life Span:	About 12 years
Personality:	Affectionate, alert, playful

Best in Show

What makes a great French bulldog? Every owner knows that his or her dog is special. Judges in dog shows, however, look very carefully at a French bulldog's appearance and behavior. Here are some of the things they look for:

large, square head and eyes that are set far apart

"bat" ears that stand straight up

short, smooth coat

pushed-in face with short nose

muzzle that is square and short

muscular body with large bones

Behavior: well behaved, curious, and alert

Glossary

abandoned (uh-BAN-duhnd) left alone and uncared for; deserted

American Kennel Club (uh-MER-i-kuhn KEN-uhl KLUHB) a national organization that is involved in many activities having to do with dogs, including collecting information about dog breeds, registering purebred dogs, and setting rules for dog shows

bonobo (buh-NOH-boh) a type of ape that looks like a small chimpanzee

bred (BRED) mated dogs from specific breeds to produce young with certain characteristics

breed (BREED) a kind of dog

brindle (BRIN-duhl) a mixture of dark and light hairs arranged in rows or bands

canine (KAY-nine) having to do with dogs

captivity (kap-TIV-uh-*tee*) a place where an animal lives that is not its natural home and where it cannot travel freely

companions (kuhm-PAN-yuhnz) animals or people who spend time with someone

fawn (FAWN) a tan color that ranges from a deep red to a pale cream

groomed (GROOMD) when an animal is kept neat and clean

Industrial Revolution (in-DUHSS-tree-uhl *rev*-uh-LOO-shuhn) a period in the late 1700s and early 1800s when people began to build factories and produce a large amount of goods; it began in Europe and then spread to North America

infections (in-FEK-shuhnz) illnesses caused by germs or viruses

joints (JOINTS) places in the body where two bones meet

kayak (KYE-ak) a covered narrow boat with a small opening in the center in which a person moves through the water by paddling

lace makers (LAYSS MAKE-uhrz) people who make a kind of cloth that has a pattern of small holes and delicate stitches

lapdogs (LAP-dawgz) small dogs that can be held in a person's lap

life jackets (LIFE JAK-its) special jackets that keep animals or people afloat in the water

litter (LIT-ur) a group of baby animals, such as puppies or kittens, that are born to the same mother at the same time

mischievous (MISS-chuh-vuhss) able to cause trouble, often through playful behavior

orangutan (uh-RANG-uh-*tan*) a large reddish-brown ape with very strong arms

orphaned (OR-fuhnd) left without parents

patient (PAY-shuhnt) good at putting up with problems without getting upset

stout (STOUT) strong and sturdy

stubborn (STUHB-urn) not willing to change or give in

veterinarian (*vet*-ur-uh-NAIR-ee-uhn) a doctor who cares for animals

Bibliography

Dannel, Kathy. *The French Bulldog: An Owner's Guide to a Happy, Healthy Pet.* Foster City, CA: Howell Book House (2000).

Lee, Muriel. *The French Bulldog: A Complete and Reliable Handbook.* Neptune City, NJ: T.F.H. (2000).

American Kennel Club
www.akc.org/breeds/french_bulldog/index.cfm

French Bull Dog Club of America
www.frenchbulldogclub.org/

Read More

Jones, Amanda. *Frenchie Kisses.* New York: Berkley Books (2010).

Montrose, Sharon. *French Bulldogs: Lightweights Littermates.* New York: Stewart, Tabori and Chang (2007).

Learn More Online

To learn more about French bulldogs, visit
www.bearportpublishing.com/LittleDogsRockII

31

Index

About the Author

Joyce Markovics is an editor, writer, and orchid collector. She lives with her husband, Adam, and an eel-shaped amphibian named Merrylegs. She hopes to get a furry pet in the near future to keep Merrylegs company.